# Contents

| | |
|---|---|
| Nature's Wonders | 1 |
| Ornate Flying Snake | 6 |
| Galaxy Frog | 10 |
| Golden Langur | 14 |
| Red Panda | 18 |
| Oriental Dwarf Kingfisher | 22 |
| Himalayan Monal | 26 |
| Orange Oakleaf Butterfly | 30 |
| Asian Glass Lizards | 34 |
| Jewel Beetle | 38 |
| Malabar Gliding Frog | 42 |
| Spot Them Here! | 46 |
| Fact Finder and Credits | 47 |

# Nature's Wonders

From the snow-capped, dry deserts of the high Himalayas, to the lush, dense jungles of the Western Ghats, India has it all. It's no surprise that each ecosystem is home to some of the most visually stunning creatures on Earth. The glint of a beetle's shell. The soft fluff of a monkey's fur. The iridescence of bird and butterfly wings. India truly has some of the world's most beautiful animals. But beauty in the wild isn't just for show – it's a matter of survival.

*Orange oakleaf butterflies are found in the Himalayas*

## Why Do Some Animals Blend In?

Hiding, or camouflage, is a simple survival strategy. For animals that are hunted, not being found is key. Take the oakleaf butterfly, whose wings help it blend seamlessly into the forest floor. By evading predators, they live to see another day. Hiding can be just as important for predators, too. Tigers mostly hunt in grasslands, scrub or dry forests. While moving, they seem to dissolve into the grass. Camouflage could mean the difference between finding a meal and going hungry.

## Then Why Do Some Animals Stand Out?

Sometimes, beauty can be an important warning. Snakes, frogs or insects that have bright colours signal danger to potential predators. They're saying, "I could be poisonous, or venomous! Wouldn't you rather eat something else?" Other animals occasionally make bold bluffs, being colourful but not venomous. They might closely mimic another species that is dangerous. Since the wrong choice can be deadly, predators often avoid making the choice at all.

## Can Beauty Attract a Mate?

Looking good takes time and effort. The same is true for animals. Colourful feathers, long tails and bright fur are hard to grow. It's a sign that these animals are so healthy that they not only survive, but also thrive. It shows potential partners that they'd be a good choice and the offspring are likely to be healthy, too. Birds are famous for their showy displays and colours. Most often, the males are beautiful, while the less colourful females sit back and choose.

*A stunning Himalayan monal in flight*

## Why Do Some Animals Shimmer Like Rainbows?

Our hair, skin and eyes are coloured by pigments. These are chemicals inside our cells that give us colour by absorbing some lights and reflecting others. Some animals don't have pigments, but rely entirely on structure. Microscopic structures bend and scatter light, producing shifting hues that dazzle or confuse predators and impress mates.

*Red pandas can be seen in the eastern reaches of the Himalayas*

# Ornate Flying Snake

**Find Me Here!**

This snake is most common in the Western Ghats, Eastern Ghats and the eastern Himalayan states.

## CRITTER STATS

**Scientific name:** *Chrysopelea ornata*
**Size:** 1–1.3 m – about the length of a guitar
**Weight:** unknown
**Lifespan:** 10 years
**Habitat:** dense tree canopies of wet forests
**Conservation status:** least concern

**This elusive and beautiful snake hangs out in the canopies of massive trees in rainforests. Good climbers, ornate flying snakes live most of their lives in treetops, ambushing frogs, geckoes and, occasionally, small birds.**

The ornate flying snake is a living optical illusion. Is it black on green or green on black? Every so often, there's a flash of red.

Its intricate design makes the snake almost impossible to pick out on the rough tree bark. Combine this with the green and black on the snake's back, and it becomes a master of camouflage.

When an unsuspecting small animal passes by, it lunges from its hiding spot to snap it up. They have fangs at the back of their mouths. The mild venom helps them hunt prey, but is not fatal to humans.

Although they're called flying snakes, they're more like really excellent gliders. They flatten their bodies into a ribbon shape and swing from side to side.

The movement allows controlled glides between trees. These snakes can even change direction mid-glide.

## DID YOU KNOW?

During the monsoon, multiple snakes entwine together to form a "mating ball". These balls can have as many as six snakes, fighting it out.

Unfortunately, these elegant snakes are threatened by the pet trade. Exotic pet traders capture and sell them, even though this is illegal.

These snakes can glide forward by as much as 100 m. That's a hundred times their body length. True long jump champs!

# Galaxy Frog

**Find Me Here!**

The galaxy frog is only found in the wet evergreen forests of the southern Western Ghats.

## CRITTER STATS
**Scientific name:** *Melanobatrachus indicus*
**Size:** 2–3 cm – the length of your knuckle!
**Weight:** up to 20 g
**Lifespan:** undocumented
**Habitat:** wet evergreen forests
**Conservation status:** vulnerable

If you're ever walking in the Western Ghats, let this frog be a reminder to keep an eye on the ground. This tiny creature hides in leaf litter, rocks and other ground cover and, unlike most frogs, it doesn't croak or sing. Since it's so hard to find, scientists know very little about it.

This spectacular frog is jet black. Its back is speckled with bright blue or whitish dots. Around the front legs are small patches of orange.

The evolution of this frog is something of a mystery. Very few frogs in India, or anywhere in the world, look anything like it.

Scientists think the galaxy frog is related to a species in Africa, but has been evolving on its own in India for the last 66 million years.

This species hails from a family of frogs called *Microhylid*, which means "narrow mouth". The narrow mouth means they hunt small ants and termites, but the exact diet of the galaxy frog is still unknown.

But why are they so spectacular to look at? Scientists think that their stunning looks might help in communication.

# DID YOU KNOW?

The Mathikettan Shola National Park in Kerala has declared the galaxy frog a "flagship species" to help protect the park.

The mysterious galaxy frog has slipped in and out of scientific history. It was first discovered in 1878, but only properly described 1997.

This frog has celebrity friends! Hollywood actor Leonardo DiCaprio once shared a stunning snap of the galaxy frog on Instagram and X. He is an ardent wildlife enthusiast.

# Golden Langur

## Find Me Here!

Found in only a small pocket of the world, from western Assam to the foothills of the Black Mountains in Bhutan.

## CRITTER STATS

**Scientific name:** *Trachypithecus geei*
**Size:** 85–95 cm (excluding tail) – like a backpack
**Weight:** 9–12 kg
**Lifespan:** 18–30 years
**Habitat:** evergreen and tropical deciduous forests
**Conservation status:** endangered

With soft, gold fur and eyes like melted chocolate, it's difficult to not be captivated by the golden langur. These monkeys hang out in groups of eight to 22. They feed often, tails dangling down from treetops like pendulums swinging in the breeze.

Pale yellow, cream, blonde, golden – the dazzling colours of the golden langur are captivating! In the sunlight, they almost seem to glow.

Their coats are creamy in the summer and darken to a golden-brown in the winter. It's possible that it helps them hide in sunlit canopies.

Around their heads, their fur tufts out like a lion's mane. Dark skin on the face, hands and feet protect langurs from sunburn.

Golden langurs hop from tree to tree, descending to the ground only very rarely.

During monsoon, they even drink rainwater and dew, never looking for ponds or lakes. Everything they need is in the trees!

# DID YOU KNOW?

Golden langurs groups usually have only one male, with multiple females.

Their stomachs are divided into multiple chambers to digest their fibre-rich diet of fruits, seeds, buds, flowers and leaves.

In many Himalayan communities, golden langurs are seen as guardians of the forests. They are worshipped as sacred creatures.

# Red Panda

## Find Me Here!

The red panda is found in the forests of the eastern Himalayas.

### CRITTER STATS

**Scientific name:** *Ailurus fulgens*
**Size:** 50–60 cm – a large pizza box
**Weight:** 3–6.5 kg
**Lifespan:** up to 23 years in captivity
**Habitat:** forests with bamboo patches
**Conservation status:** endangered

*Some of the images in this chapter are of red pandas from other countries*

Don't let the name fool you! While they might be cute and cuddly like giant pandas, red pandas are closely related to skunks and weasels. The red panda is fiery in colour, quiet in nature and full of surprises you'd never expect.

The red panda's body is covered in dense, dark red fur, while the tip of its tail and underbelly are reddish-brown. Its face gives it an adorable, cartoon-like appearance!

The red panda's white ears, eyebrows and whiskers could have evolved to reflect light, keeping the sun out of their eyes.

Why is it called panda even though the giant panda and red panda aren't closely related? Their diets are where the similarities come from.

Both eat bamboo and have developed mitten-shaped paws with thumbs to grasp bamboo. This allows them to grab and break bamboo, reaching the shoots within.

These thumbs are also great for grasping tree bark. They can scurry up and down trees to escape predators and sunbathe in the winter.

# DID YOU KNOW?

Although you're more likely to see a red panda than hear one, they do make noises. They squeal, twitter, huff, hiss and grunt!

Red pandas make their nests high up in trees. Females can give birth to up to four cubs, usually during the summer.

They use scent to mark territories. They secrete chemicals through the pads of their paws, leaving a scent behind, as they climb up and down trees.

# Oriental Dwarf Kingfisher

**Find Me Here!**

Found across the forests of the Western Ghats.

### CRITTER STATS
**Scientific name:** *Ceyx erithaca*
**Size:** 12.5–14 cm – the length of your hand
**Weight:** 14–21 g
**Lifespan:** approximately 4 years
**Habitat:** forested areas near streams and ponds
**Conservation status:** near threatened

The Oriental dwarf kingfisher is so colourful that it looks like it was designed by an artist! Also called the black-backed dwarf kingfisher, this tiny bird is a jewel of the forest, rarely seen, but unforgettable once spotted.

The bird's stomach is a bright, electric orange – like a spark from a fire. The bird's head is a bright pink and bill is even brighter!

The kingfisher's wings are an iridescent bluish purple. When it takes flight and the wings beat, the colours seem to blend into one.

Interestingly, this blend of colours is not used to attract a mate. Unlike most birds, the females and the males look almost identical. Scientists aren't quite sure why this bird looks like a rainbow in flight.

Although it's called a kingfisher, its diet is not all fish. It eats mostly insects, like grasshoppers, beetles, mantises and ants.

When they do hunt fish, they just skim the surface of the water, grabbing fish with their toes. It's known as the dwarf kingfisher since it's much smaller than its other kingfisher siblings.

#  DID YOU KNOW?

The black-backed dwarf kingfisher nests underground. The male and female work together to dig a tunnel, and lay their eggs inside.

For most of the year, this bird is solitary, foraging and perching alone. They form pairs during breeding season, and join large flocks when migrating.

Once it spots its prey and dives, the black-backed dwarf kingfisher can reach speeds of up to 40 km/h.

# Himalayan Monal

## Find Me Here!

As the name suggests, this bird lives in the Indian Himalayan region, from Jammu and Kashmir to Arunachal Pradesh.

### CRITTER STATS
**Family:** *Lophophorus impejanus*
**Size:** about 70 cm – the width of a school desk
**Weight:** a little over 2 kg
**Lifespan:** 10–12 years
**Habitat:** high-altitude forests and grasslands
**Conservation status:** least concern

The Himalayan monal is a burst of colour in the stark Himalayan landscape of white, greys and browns. This impressive bird is the national bird of Nepal as well as the state bird of Himachal Pradesh.

Adult male birds are adorned with a metallic green crown fit for a king. Their heads are greenish and the wings are particularly spectacular!

The shining shades of blue and purple on its back and wings turn to a warm, sunset orange near the bird's tail.

In contrast to the splendid male, the female is quite plain. These birds don't live in pairs.

It is a polygamous species, which means that the male has many partners. But he has to work hard to win them!

He puts on an elaborate display, stretching out his wings and tail and lowering his head. A dozen males are sometimes found displaying near nesting areas.

# DID YOU KNOW?

Himalayan monals have an impressive range of calls and body displays. They express contentment, aggression, alarm and even advertise for mates using vocal and body language.

In the winters, most plant matter is buried under snow and ice. They use their strong beaks and claws to look for food up to 10 inches below the ground.

Monals (*Lophophorus impejanus*) are named after Lady Mary Impey, the wife of a British chief justice of Bengal in the 18th century. She was said to have kept monals in her aviary.

# Orange Oakleaf Butterfly

## Find Me Here!

The orange oakleaf butterfly is found in the forests of the Himalayan region.

### CRITTER STATS

**Family:** *Kallima inachus*
**Size:** 8–11 cm – the length of a smartphone
**Weight:** unknown, likely less than a gram
**Lifespan:** 45–54 days
**Habitat:** mid- to high- altitude oak-pine forests
**Conservation status:** unknown

The orange oakleaf butterfly lives in the quiet corners of forests. It is quite a shape-shifter – one moment a dead leaf, the next a flash of vivid orange and blue!

The orange oakleaf is a master of camouflage. When the wings are closed, the orange oakleaf looks almost exactly like a dry leaf.

It has a mottled, light brown appearance. Its wings' shape and texture is even more impressive! They even have veins like real leaves.

When the wings are open, the butterfly suddenly comes alive. The wings are a rich, royal bluish violet with bright stripes of orange.

This butterfly also changes colours with the seasons. In the dry season, the rich blues fade to a softer violet so as not to stand out in the dry, largely brown leaf litter.

It is also a little larger during the dry months. It seems to be less active then and might rely on this large-leaf camouflage more.

# DID YOU KNOW?

The oakleaf's wings have eyespots, which can startle predators like birds. It makes the butterfly look like a bigger animal!

If the female butterflies are well fed, they can lay up to 300 eggs every season.

A citizen's poll elected the orange oakleaf as India's national butterfly in October 2020.

# Asian Glass Lizards

**Find Me Here!**

The Asian glass lizard lives in the eastern Himalaya states.

### CRITTER STATS
**Family:** *Dopasia gracilis*
**Size:** up to 45 cm – the length of two textbooks
**Weight:** unknown, but similarly sized glass lizards weigh 300–600 g
**Lifespan:** unknown
**Habitat:** dense leaf litter in forests
**Conservation status:** least concern

Lizard or snake? Actually, it's a legless lizard! The Asian glass lizard is part of a family of burrowing lizards that have lost their legs as they evolved over millions of years. It lives most of its life underground and shines under the light only for brief moments.

It's called the "glass" lizard due to its sparkling appearance. The tiny scales shimmer underneath light, making it glow orange.

Across its body are electric blue bands, stopping just before the tail. The colours help in defence as they signal danger to a predator.

They also confuse predators, making them focus on the less brightly coloured tail instead (and this is a clever plan – read on)!

Like other lizards, the Asian glass lizard doesn't mind letting go of its tail. When a predator attacks, the lizard detaches its tail – leaving it behind with the confused predator – and makes a run for it.

Young glass lizards don't have these spectacular colours. They are a soft cream with black stripes.

# DID YOU KNOW?

Asian glass lizards reproduce through eggs. Females lay between 5 and 15 eggs in an underground burrow and they take a few months to hatch.

This lizard's tail makes up two-thirds of its body!

Its snake-like appearance and bright colours often confuses people, making them think the glass lizard is a deadly snake. But this lizard is definitively venom-free.

# Jewel Beetle

### Find Me Here!

Different types of jewel beetles are found all over India.

## CRITTER STATS

**Scientific name:** *Buprestidae*
**Size:** 3–80 mm – the height of a one-rupee coin, or as long as your thumb
**Weight:** a few grams at most
**Lifespan:** 1 or 2 days–2 weeks
**Habitat:** trees or woody shrubs
**Conservation status:** unknown

*Some of the images in this chapter are of jewel beetles from other countries*

Unlike the other species in this book, the jewel beetles are actually an entire family! There are over 15,000 varieties of these beautiful beetles across the world. Each one is famous for a greenish-blue hue, which changes colour under sunlight. They truly are a jewel amongst insects.

Have you ever held a CD up to the light and watched it change colours? As it moves, it shimmers with rainbows. CDs are actually covered in millions of little grooves.

The wings of the jewel beetle are covered in similar tiny grooves. In fact, jewel beetle wings act exactly like a CD!

Sunlight, which is made up of seven colours, bounces off the grooves in multiple directions. The colours then separate and fan out.

It's the play of light, called structural colours, that creates the dazzling hues of the jewel beetle. These tiny bugs have figured out all of the tricks of light!

The iridescent colours confuse predators, making structural colour a spectacular form of camouflage. Jewel beetles blend in by standing out.

#  DID YOU KNOW?

Beetlewing craft refers to the tradition of using jewel beetle wings to decorate clothes and artwork. The Mughals were known to sew the wings onto robes.

Some species of jewel beetles are threatened by insect collectors. They are so prized that they have begun to disappear from the wild.

Jewel beetles aren't born this beautiful. They spend weeks as tiny, white, maggot-like larvae, eating plants and getting strong enough to transform.

# Malabar Gliding Frog

**Find Me Here!**

This is an endemic species – it is found only in the Western Ghats and nowhere else in the world!

### CRITTER STATS
**Scientific name:** *Rhacophorus malabaricus*
**Size:** up to 8 cm – like a small chocolate bar
**Weight:** unknown, likely 0.6–1.2 g, like other similarly sized frogs
**Lifespan:** unknown
**Habitat:** dense forests with thick canopies
**Conservation status:** least concern

It's a bird! It's a plane! No – it's a frog! These excellent climbers jump from canopy to canopy, using their webbed feet to catch the air and glide for up to 10 m at a time. That's 118 times their body length!

We usually associate frogs with ponds or lakes. Tree frogs live a different life. They must balance their need for water with the safety of tree canopies.

Water is scarce in treetops. Climbing up and down giant jungle trees is a tough feat for a tiny frog. Scientists think gliding reduces the time it takes for them to reach water.

The Malabar gliding frog has webbed toes that catch air and help them glide – the fast way to travel in a dense forest! This webbing is a bright-electric orange and stands out vividly.

The rest of the body is two-toned. On top, they are bright green and underneath, these frogs are a lighter yellow-white.

This helps them blend into their habitat and make them hard to spot between the greens and yellows of jungle trees.

#  DID YOU KNOW?

Tadpoles of this species are born into a bubble bath. Females make a foam nest of bubbles and lay eggs inside.

They suspend these nests above water bodies. Once the eggs hatch, the tadpoles fall into the water, ready to grow into a frog.

Female Malabar gliding frogs are much larger than males! During the breeding season, multiple males compete for the largest females in a group.

# Spot Them Here!

Follow the pug marks to find some of the best places to spot India's amazing wildlife! Animals such as jewel beetles live across many regions of India and can be spotted quite close to home, too.

## Fact Finder

"AmphibiaWeb - Microhylidae." https://amphibiaweb.org/lists/Microhylidae.shtml.

"Black-Backed Dwarf-Kingfisher (Oriental Dwarf Kingfisher)." *eBird*. https://ebird.org/species/bkbkin1..

Chatterjee, Upayan. "A Walk Across Tiger Country In Search Of India's National Butterfly." *Roundglass Sustain*, https://roundglasssustain.com/habitats/pakke-oakleaf.

Crew, Bec. "Oriental Dwarf Kingfisher, a Rainbow by Any Other Name." *Australian Geographic*, 22 May 2014, https://www.australiangeographic.com.au/blogs/creatura-blog/2014/05/oriental-dwarf-kingfisher/.

"Galaxy Frog." *EDGE of Existence*, https://www.edgeofexistence.org/species/galaxy-frog/.

"Gee's Golden Langur - Facts, Diet, Habitat & Pictures." *Animalia.Bio*. https://animalia.bio/gees-golden-langur/1000.

"Golden Tree Snake (Snakes Of Peninsular India)." *iNaturalist*. iNaturalist, https://www.inaturalist.org/guide_taxa/1331753.

"Jewel Beetle." *The Australian Museum*, https://australian.museum/learn/animals/insects/jewel-beetle/.

Martin, Gerry. "Asian Glass Lizard: Jewel-Toned Enigma from the Northeast." *Roundglass Sustain*, https://roundglasssustain.com/species/asian-glass-lizard.

Nisarg Prakash. "Malabar Gliding Frog: Habitat, Breeding, Threats." *Roundglass Sustain*, https://roundglasssustain.com/infographics/malabar-gliding-frog-facts.

"Orange Oakleaf (Kallima Inachus)." *iNaturalist*, https://www.inaturalist.org/taxa/67980-Kallima-inachus.

Palit, Shubham. "The Curious Mating Ritual Of Ornate Flying Snakes." *Nature in Focus*, https://www.natureinfocus.in/animals/the-curious-mating-ritual-of-ornate-flying-snakes.

Prakash, Nisarg. "Asian Glass Lizard: Facts, Habitat, Range." *Roundglass Sustain*, https://roundglasssustain.com/infographics/asian-glass-lizard-facts.

"Red Panda." *Smithsonian's National Zoo and Conservation Biology Institute*, https://nationalzoo.si.edu/animals/red-panda.

Seshadri, K.S. "High Life: Gliding Frogs of the Western Ghats." *Roundglass Sustain*. https://roundglasssustain.com/species/high-life-gliding-frogs-western-ghats.

## Credits

**Writer:** Yamini Srikanth

**Designer:** Bandana Paul

**Picture Credits**

**iStockphoto:** ePhotocorp, #1164856425; Niels Christian Madsen, #2173653848; Niels Christian Madsen, #2173488983; Danielrao, #1301000549; vyasphoto, #1333722058; gui000878, #588354646; EyeEm Mobile GmbH, #2171673618; Ljs photography, Birmingham, U.K., #1132837061; Zocha_K, #2010552821; Zocha_K, #1263025199; PrinPrince, #658800060; BirdHunter591, #1251302267; sutiporn, #958771610; BirdHunter591, #1159122821; PrinPrince, #1019184510; Thamrongrat Tanomtham, #1160506658; jbhavya, #2188157981; Ranzi Photography, #2211565668; Sushil Bisht, #1326195938; ePhotocorp, #1286090764; Adisak Mitrprayoon, #1450620535; EyeEm Mobile GmbH, #2197720861; 49pauly, #1262297271; teptong, #880782552; Wirestock, #1447860875; Jayantibhai Movaliya, #2181786743; Aniful Izza, #1962474166; ePhotocorp, #1358187398; Jayantibhai Movaliya, #2162010322; pixbox77, #1056455412; ePhotocorp, #1464047592; Raghu_Ramaswamy, #1057171064; Anand RJ, #1411054333; ePhotocorp, #1004714804; ePhotocorp, #1263782289; Raghu_Ramaswamy, #1057170976.

**iNaturalist:** Galaxy Frog (Melanobatrachus indicus) by rajesh rocky; Galaxy Frog (Melanobatrachus indicus) by rajesh rocky; Asian Glass Lizard (Dopasia gracilis) by Rohit; Asian Glass Lizard (Dopasia gracilis) by Rohit; Asian Glass Lizard (Dopasia gracilis) by Daniel J. Layton; Asian Glass Lizard (Dopasia gracilis) by Devin.

**Wikimedia Commons:** Chrysopelea ornata by AshLin; Photo of Golden Tree Snake by rejilkrishna_pr; Flying snake (Chrysopelea ornata) by Dr.R.S.Pradeep Raj; Chrysopelea ornata by Len Worthington; Chrysopelea ornata by Shagil Kannur; Chrysopelea ornata in Kannur by Shagil Kannur; melanobatrachus indicus by Davidvraju; melanobatrachus indicus by Davidvraju; Melanobatrachus indicus India Western by Ben tapley; Melanobatrachus indicus by Sandeep Das; Malabar black narrow-mouthed Frog by Drjpmenon; melanobatrachus indicus by Davidvraju; At Kakoijana WR by Jugal Bharali; Gee's Golden Lutung (Trachypithecus geei) by kalyanvarma; Golden langur by Ekabhishek; Golden Langur by Rohit Naniwadekar; Gee's Golden Lutung (Trachypithecus geei) by kalyanvarma; Golden langur with infant by Krunal Desai - Wildlife Photography; Golden langur in Assam by Yathin S Krishnappa; Ceyx erithaca by Pkhun; Oriental dwarf kingfisher by Anup Deodhar; Lophophorus impejanus HIMALAYAN MONAL by NasserHalaweh; Himalayan Monal Lophophorus impejanus in flight by Mildeep; Himalayan Monal, male, Bhulkan, Uttarakhand, India by Mike Prince; Himalayan Monal Pangolakha Wildlife Sanctuary East Sikkim India by Dibyendu Ash; Orange Oakleaf Kallima inachus by Dr. Raju Kasambe; Orange Oakleaf WLB by Rijuroy89; Asian Glass Lizard (Dopasia gracilis) in India by Subhadra Devi; Buprestidae by Katunchi; Rhacophorus malabaricus by Vinayaraj; Foam nest created by Malabar Gliding Frogs by Arpita Dutta; Malabar Gliding Frog Pair by Nireekshit; Golden Langur @ Assam by M.Swarnali.

**Independent Sources:** Red panda and *Melanobatrachus indicus* images by Shashank Dalvi.

**Map:** Syailendra Gupta Muliawan, India Vectors by Vecteezy.

First published by Juggernaut Books 2025

Text copyright © Juggernaut Books 2025

10 9 8 7 6 5 4 3 2 1

P-ISBN: 9789353454074

E-ISBN: 9789353453756

All rights reserved. No part of this publication may be reproduced, transmitted, or stored in a retrieval system in any form or by any means without the written permission of the publisher.

Printed at Nutech Print Services - India